# THE ART OF

# GRATITUDE

## 3 MINUTE MORNING RITUAL JOURNAL

BY

NAZANIN MANDI

T0019441

RISE WITH *PURPOSE.*
MOVE WITH *GRATITUDE.*
SLEEP IN *PEACE.*

# INTRODUCTION.

Depression and anxiety are concealed by many faces—most of which are never the truth about what's residing within. Hiding the fact is draining and pretending to be jovial is not only deceiving, but harmful to one's overall well-being. I spent most of my 20's in deep-seated denial, rooted in depression. Lost, entangled in a new lifestyle that never aligned with my personal truth, heartbroken over my parents' divorce after 23 years, battling body dysmorphia, fighting the fear of unfulfilled potential but too scared to do anything about it, living in the shadows; a personal choice, always hesitant to speak my mind and live out loud. It got to a point where I was repulsed by my own bullshit. So uncomfortable with how deep my depression had gotten, that I was now more than willing to be twice as uncomfortable to change for the better. So I began to write a list; instead of writing down all the things I wanted to modify in my life, I wrote down everything I was already grateful for to help motivate and kick-start my evolution. For me, gratitude is the foundation of hope, faith and the pursuit of personal fulfilment. When we are aware of what we already possess, we can build better with confidence. Along with therapy and some very honest conversations with myself, I began to be present and find joy in the journey instead of being discouraged and so hard on myself every step of the way. The work is never-ending but so is gratitude. Show gratitude for your abilities, opportunities and time granted. Never forget there is delight in the voyage but *gratitude is key*.

—

XOXO

Gratitude is a state of being.
Gratitude starts from within.
Gratitude motivates manifestation.

When we are grateful for what we already have, we attract our highest potential. But achieving everything we desire also must be followed by action.

**EVERYTHING IS INTERCONNECTED.**

# AFFIRMATION.

"I,_____,
am focused on my needs, wants, and personal goals. I will remain committed to the journey but also flexible in my approach. I understand nothing worthwhile comes easy, and success ebbs and flows. I make a promise to myself to move with grace, confidence, integrity, and faith.

## I GOT THIS!"

# A MESSAGE
# FROM THE AUTHOR.

Are you currently on your quest for self-discovery? I truly believe we all are, to some capacity ... Self-fulfillment ebbs and flows, requiring nurture throughout every stage of our lives. Recharge is essential, so I am on a mission to help you find balance and to evoke gratefulness for everything you already receive. Currently, I am at a place in life where I look at each day as a new and exciting opportunity to better myself, my surroundings, and the things I attract—and I hope to motivate you to feel and do the same. When we move with gratitude, we are a magnetic force that knows no bounds when attaining whatever our heart desires. Remember, every sunrise is a redo, and every sunset is a recharge ... there are no bad days, just lessons learned which will lead to brighter places.

—
Nazanin Mandi
xoxo

# I AM A WORK IN PROGRESS AND CURRENTLY ON THE PURSUIT OF PEACE AND NOT JUST HAPPINESS.

---

Confidence, class, and grace can defy ANY sort of
doubt or worry you carry with you on the daily.
Hope over fear ... Action over inactive.

| I AM *GRATEFUL* FOR ... | DATE: |
|---|---|

1. _____
2. _____
3. _____

| I AM *GRATEFUL* FOR ... | DATE: |
|---|---|

1. _____
2. _____
3. _____

| I AM *GRATEFUL* FOR ... | DATE: |
|---|---|

1. _____
2. _____
3. _____

| I AM *GRATEFUL* FOR ... | DATE: |
|---|---|

1. _____
2. _____
3. _____

| I AM *GRATEFUL* FOR ... | DATE: |
|---|---|

1. _____
2. _____
3. _____

| I AM *GRATEFUL* FOR ... | DATE: |
|---|---|

1. _____
2. _____
3. _____

| I AM *GRATEFUL* FOR ... | DATE: |
|---|---|

1. _____
2. _____
3. _____

# I AM A WORK IN PROGRESS AND CURRENTLY ON THE PURSUIT OF PEACE AND NOT JUST HAPPINESS.

---

May we all be strong-minded and strong-willed, yet soft enough to be encouraging and kind to one another. Always xo.

| I AM *GRATEFUL* FOR ... | DATE: |
|---|---|

1. _____
2. _____
3. _____

| I AM *GRATEFUL* FOR ... | DATE: |
|---|---|

1. _____
2. _____
3. _____

| I AM *GRATEFUL* FOR ... | DATE: |
|---|---|

1. _____
2. _____
3. _____

| I AM *GRATEFUL* FOR … | DATE: |
|---|---|

1. _____
2. _____
3. _____

| I AM *GRATEFUL* FOR … | DATE: |
|---|---|

1. _____
2. _____
3. _____

| I AM *GRATEFUL* FOR … | DATE: |
|---|---|

1. _____
2. _____
3. _____

| I AM *GRATEFUL* FOR … | DATE: |
|---|---|

1. _____
2. _____
3. _____

# I AM A WORK IN PROGRESS AND CURRENTLY ON THE PURSUIT OF PEACE AND NOT JUST HAPPINESS.

There comes a point in life where you have to take accountability for the things you're not getting ... We often get so caught up and/or distracted by life that we forget we are in control of our own success.

| I AM *GRATEFUL* FOR ... | DATE: |
|---|---|

1. _____
2. _____
3. _____

| I AM *GRATEFUL* FOR ... | DATE: |
|---|---|

1. _____
2. _____
3. _____

| I AM *GRATEFUL* FOR ... | DATE: |
|---|---|

1. _____
2. _____
3. _____

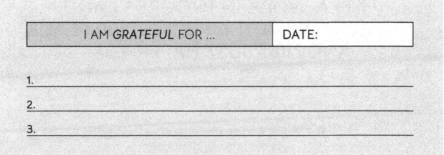

| I AM *GRATEFUL* FOR … | DATE: |
|---|---|

1. _____
2. _____
3. _____

| I AM *GRATEFUL* FOR … | DATE: |
|---|---|

1. _____
2. _____
3. _____

| I AM *GRATEFUL* FOR … | DATE: |
|---|---|

1. _____
2. _____
3. _____

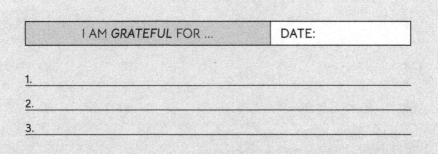

| I AM *GRATEFUL* FOR … | DATE: |
|---|---|

1. _____
2. _____
3. _____

# I AM A WORK IN PROGRESS AND CURRENTLY ON THE PURSUIT OF PEACE AND NOT JUST HAPPINESS.

---

Most of everything we worry about stems from some
type of insecurity ... Let it go.

| I AM *GRATEFUL* FOR ... | DATE: |
|---|---|

1. _____
2. _____
3. _____

| I AM *GRATEFUL* FOR ... | DATE: |
|---|---|

1. _____
2. _____
3. _____

| I AM *GRATEFUL* FOR ... | DATE: |
|---|---|

1. _____
2. _____
3. _____

| I AM *GRATEFUL* FOR ... | DATE: |
|---|---|

1. _____
2. _____
3. _____

| I AM *GRATEFUL* FOR ... | DATE: |
|---|---|

1. _____
2. _____
3. _____

| I AM *GRATEFUL* FOR ... | DATE: |
|---|---|

1. _____
2. _____
3. _____

| I AM *GRATEFUL* FOR ... | DATE: |
|---|---|

1. _____
2. _____
3. _____

EVERY TRIUMPH
SHOULD BE
CELEBRATED
BIG OR SMALL.
IF IT PUSHED YOU
AND/OR BROUGHT
YOU JOY,
MAKE IT KNOWN.

# WHO ARE YOU MOST GRATEFUL FOR
# IN YOUR LIFE AND WHY?

_____

_____

_____

_____

_____

_____

_____

_____

_____

_____

_____

_____

_____

_____

_____

_____

_____

# I AM A WORK IN PROGRESS AND CURRENTLY ON THE PURSUIT OF PEACE AND NOT JUST HAPPINESS.

Did you do at least one thing for yourself today that will better your tomorrow?

| I AM *GRATEFUL* FOR ... | DATE: |
|---|---|

1. _____
2. _____
3. _____

| I AM *GRATEFUL* FOR ... | DATE: |
|---|---|

1. _____
2. _____
3. _____

| I AM *GRATEFUL* FOR ... | DATE: |
|---|---|

1. _____
2. _____
3. _____

| I AM *GRATEFUL* FOR ... | DATE: |
|---|---|

1. _____
2. _____
3. _____

| I AM *GRATEFUL* FOR ... | DATE: |
|---|---|

1. _____
2. _____
3. _____

| I AM *GRATEFUL* FOR ... | DATE: |
|---|---|

1. _____
2. _____
3. _____

| I AM *GRATEFUL* FOR ... | DATE: |
|---|---|

1. _____
2. _____
3. _____

# I AM A WORK IN PROGRESS AND CURRENTLY ON THE PURSUIT OF PEACE AND NOT JUST HAPPINESS.

We are all multifaceted beings, constantly evolving. Our many qualities are proof that as individuals, we can have and juggle it all. Embrace those juxtaposed expectations, even if it makes others uncomfortable.

| I AM *GRATEFUL* FOR ... | DATE: |
|---|---|

1. _____
2. _____
3. _____

| I AM *GRATEFUL* FOR ... | DATE: |
|---|---|

1. _____
2. _____
3. _____

| I AM *GRATEFUL* FOR ... | DATE: |
|---|---|

1. _____
2. _____
3. _____

| I AM *GRATEFUL* FOR ... | DATE: |
|---|---|

1. _____
2. _____
3. _____

| I AM *GRATEFUL* FOR ... | DATE: |
|---|---|

1. _____
2. _____
3. _____

| I AM *GRATEFUL* FOR ... | DATE: |
|---|---|

1. _____
2. _____
3. _____

| I AM *GRATEFUL* FOR ... | DATE: |
|---|---|

1. _____
2. _____
3. _____

# I AM A WORK IN PROGRESS AND CURRENTLY ON THE PURSUIT OF PEACE AND NOT JUST HAPPINESS.

Growth requires growing pains, and being uncomfortable leads to some beautiful, colorful destinations.

| I AM *GRATEFUL* FOR ... | DATE: |
|---|---|

1. _____
2. _____
3. _____

| I AM *GRATEFUL* FOR ... | DATE: |
|---|---|

1. _____
2. _____
3. _____

| I AM *GRATEFUL* FOR ... | DATE: |
|---|---|

1. _____
2. _____
3. _____

| I AM *GRATEFUL* FOR … | DATE: |
|---|---|

1. _____
2. _____
3. _____

| I AM *GRATEFUL* FOR … | DATE: |
|---|---|

1. _____
2. _____
3. _____

| I AM *GRATEFUL* FOR … | DATE: |
|---|---|

1. _____
2. _____
3. _____

| I AM *GRATEFUL* FOR … | DATE: |
|---|---|

1. _____
2. _____
3. _____

# I AM A WORK IN PROGRESS AND CURRENTLY ON THE PURSUIT OF PEACE AND NOT JUST HAPPINESS.

---

You don't have to like everything about yourself.
You just have to own it.

| I AM *GRATEFUL* FOR ... | DATE: |
|---|---|

1. _____
2. _____
3. _____

| I AM *GRATEFUL* FOR ... | DATE: |
|---|---|

1. _____
2. _____
3. _____

| I AM *GRATEFUL* FOR ... | DATE: |
|---|---|

1. _____
2. _____
3. _____

| I AM *GRATEFUL* FOR ... | DATE: |
|---|---|

1. _____
2. _____
3. _____

| I AM *GRATEFUL* FOR ... | DATE: |
|---|---|

1. _____
2. _____
3. _____

| I AM *GRATEFUL* FOR ... | DATE: |
|---|---|

1. _____
2. _____
3. _____

| I AM *GRATEFUL* FOR ... | DATE: |
|---|---|

1. _____
2. _____
3. _____

EVERYTHING
WE WANT
AND ARE GOING
THROUGH
IS PREPARING US
FOR SOMETHING
GREAT.

# WHAT ARE THE TOP 3 PLACES YOU'VE BEEN TO THAT BRING YOU PEACE?

(THINK OF THEM OFTEN)

_____

_____

_____

_____

_____

_____

_____

_____

_____

_____

_____

_____

_____

_____

_____

_____

_____

# I AM A WORK IN PROGRESS AND CURRENTLY ON THE PURSUIT OF PEACE AND NOT JUST HAPPINESS.

---

Growth is key, but not mandatory.
It takes significant effort to evolve, and it is constant work.

| I AM *GRATEFUL* FOR ... | DATE: |
|---|---|

1. _____
2. _____
3. _____

| I AM *GRATEFUL* FOR ... | DATE: |
|---|---|

1. _____
2. _____
3. _____

| I AM *GRATEFUL* FOR ... | DATE: |
|---|---|

1. _____
2. _____
3. _____

| I AM *GRATEFUL* FOR ... | DATE: |
|---|---|

1. _____
2. _____
3. _____

| I AM *GRATEFUL* FOR ... | DATE: |
|---|---|

1. _____
2. _____
3. _____

| I AM *GRATEFUL* FOR ... | DATE: |
|---|---|

1. _____
2. _____
3. _____

| I AM *GRATEFUL* FOR ... | DATE: |
|---|---|

1. _____
2. _____
3. _____

# I AM A WORK IN PROGRESS AND CURRENTLY ON THE PURSUIT OF PEACE AND NOT JUST HAPPINESS.

---

Once we settle our ego and fears, take accountability,
and have a clear cut plan, we can all excel in anything we put our minds to.
Self-realization and admittance is the first step.

| I AM *GRATEFUL* FOR ... | DATE: |
|---|---|

1. _____
2. _____
3. _____

| I AM *GRATEFUL* FOR ... | DATE: |
|---|---|

1. _____
2. _____
3. _____

| I AM *GRATEFUL* FOR ... | DATE: |
|---|---|

1. _____
2. _____
3. _____

| I AM *GRATEFUL* FOR ... | DATE: |
|---|---|

1. _____
2. _____
3. _____

| I AM *GRATEFUL* FOR ... | DATE: |
|---|---|

1. _____
2. _____
3. _____

| I AM *GRATEFUL* FOR ... | DATE: |
|---|---|

1. _____
2. _____
3. _____

| I AM *GRATEFUL* FOR ... | DATE: |
|---|---|

1. _____
2. _____
3. _____

# I AM A WORK IN PROGRESS AND CURRENTLY ON THE PURSUIT OF PEACE AND NOT JUST HAPPINESS.

---

Why drag when we can uplift?

| I AM *GRATEFUL* FOR ... | DATE: |
|---|---|

1. _____
2. _____
3. _____

| I AM *GRATEFUL* FOR ... | DATE: |
|---|---|

1. _____
2. _____
3. _____

| I AM *GRATEFUL* FOR ... | DATE: |
|---|---|

1. _____
2. _____
3. _____

| I AM *GRATEFUL* FOR … | DATE: |
|---|---|

1. _____
2. _____
3. _____

| I AM *GRATEFUL* FOR … | DATE: |
|---|---|

1. _____
2. _____
3. _____

| I AM *GRATEFUL* FOR … | DATE: |
|---|---|

1. _____
2. _____
3. _____

| I AM *GRATEFUL* FOR … | DATE: |
|---|---|

1. _____
2. _____
3. _____

# I AM A WORK IN PROGRESS AND CURRENTLY ON THE PURSUIT OF PEACE AND NOT JUST HAPPINESS.

Why compare when we can complete?

| I AM *GRATEFUL* FOR ... | DATE: |
| --- | --- |

1. _____
2. _____
3. _____

| I AM *GRATEFUL* FOR ... | DATE: |
| --- | --- |

1. _____
2. _____
3. _____

| I AM *GRATEFUL* FOR ... | DATE: |
| --- | --- |

1. _____
2. _____
3. _____

| I AM *GRATEFUL* FOR ... | DATE: |
|---|---|

1. _____
2. _____
3. _____

| I AM *GRATEFUL* FOR ... | DATE: |
|---|---|

1. _____
2. _____
3. _____

| I AM *GRATEFUL* FOR ... | DATE: |
|---|---|

1. _____
2. _____
3. _____

| I AM *GRATEFUL* FOR ... | DATE: |
|---|---|

1. _____
2. _____
3. _____

IF YOU DON'T
BELIEVE IN THE
"MAGIC,"
YOU'LL NEVER
RECEIVE IT.

# WHAT IS YOUR PASSION, AND WHAT IS STOPPING YOU FROM PURSUING IT?

_____

_____

_____

_____

_____

_____

_____

_____

_____

_____

_____

_____

_____

_____

_____

_____

_____

_____

# I AM A WORK IN PROGRESS AND CURRENTLY ON THE PURSUIT OF PEACE AND NOT JUST HAPPINESS.

---

What we say, and put out into existence, will eventually come to fruition ONLY if we work hard and truly believe.

| I AM *GRATEFUL* FOR … | DATE: |
|---|---|

1. _____
2. _____
3. _____

| I AM *GRATEFUL* FOR … | DATE: |
|---|---|

1. _____
2. _____
3. _____

| I AM *GRATEFUL* FOR … | DATE: |
|---|---|

1. _____
2. _____
3. _____

**I AM *GRATEFUL* FOR …**     DATE:

1. _____
2. _____
3. _____

**I AM *GRATEFUL* FOR …**     DATE:

1. _____
2. _____
3. _____

**I AM *GRATEFUL* FOR …**     DATE:

1. _____
2. _____
3. _____

**I AM *GRATEFUL* FOR …**     DATE:

1. _____
2. _____
3. _____

# I AM A WORK IN PROGRESS AND CURRENTLY ON THE PURSUIT OF PEACE AND NOT JUST HAPPINESS.

---

Humbling oneself, coming to terms with your issues, and eternally working towards bettering them are sure signs that self-evolution is more than attainable.

| I AM *GRATEFUL* FOR ... | DATE: |
|---|---|

1. _____
2. _____
3. _____

| I AM *GRATEFUL* FOR ... | DATE: |
|---|---|

1. _____
2. _____
3. _____

| I AM *GRATEFUL* FOR ... | DATE: |
|---|---|

1. _____
2. _____
3. _____

| I AM *GRATEFUL* FOR … | DATE: |
| --- | --- |

1. _____
2. _____
3. _____

| I AM *GRATEFUL* FOR … | DATE: |
| --- | --- |

1. _____
2. _____
3. _____

| I AM *GRATEFUL* FOR … | DATE: |
| --- | --- |

1. _____
2. _____
3. _____

| I AM *GRATEFUL* FOR … | DATE: |
| --- | --- |

1. _____
2. _____
3. _____

# I AM A WORK IN PROGRESS AND CURRENTLY ON THE PURSUIT OF PEACE AND NOT JUST HAPPINESS.

---

Truth is, we sometimes create issues within ourselves
that aren't even relevant.

| I AM *GRATEFUL* FOR ... | DATE: |
|---|---|

1. _____
2. _____
3. _____

| I AM *GRATEFUL* FOR ... | DATE: |
|---|---|

1. _____
2. _____
3. _____

| I AM *GRATEFUL* FOR ... | DATE: |
|---|---|

1. _____
2. _____
3. _____

| I AM *GRATEFUL* FOR ... | DATE: |
|---|---|

1. _____
2. _____
3. _____

| I AM *GRATEFUL* FOR ... | DATE: |
|---|---|

1. _____
2. _____
3. _____

| I AM *GRATEFUL* FOR ... | DATE: |
|---|---|

1. _____
2. _____
3. _____

| I AM *GRATEFUL* FOR ... | DATE: |
|---|---|

1. _____
2. _____
3. _____

# I AM A WORK IN PROGRESS AND CURRENTLY ON THE PURSUIT OF PEACE AND NOT JUST HAPPINESS.

---

In times of weakness and low self-esteem, let us all
try to remember our positive attributes, qualities, and talents.
Not the things we THINK we lack.

| I AM *GRATEFUL* FOR ... | DATE: |
|---|---|

1. _____
2. _____
3. _____

| I AM *GRATEFUL* FOR ... | DATE: |
|---|---|

1. _____
2. _____
3. _____

| I AM *GRATEFUL* FOR ... | DATE: |
|---|---|

1. _____
2. _____
3. _____

| I AM *GRATEFUL* FOR … | DATE: |
|---|---|

1. _____
2. _____
3. _____

| I AM *GRATEFUL* FOR … | DATE: |
|---|---|

1. _____
2. _____
3. _____

| I AM *GRATEFUL* FOR … | DATE: |
|---|---|

1. _____
2. _____
3. _____

| I AM *GRATEFUL* FOR … | DATE: |
|---|---|

1. _____
2. _____
3. _____

APPREHENSION

ENDS

WHERE

GRATITUDE

BLOSSOMS.

# WHAT ARE YOUR TOP 3 PODCASTS
# THAT MOTIVATE YOU?

### (LISTEN TO THEM WEEKLY)

_____

_____

_____

_____

_____

_____

_____

_____

_____

_____

_____

_____

_____

_____

_____

_____

_____

_____

# I AM A WORK IN PROGRESS AND CURRENTLY ON THE PURSUIT OF PEACE AND NOT JUST HAPPINESS.

---

Not every goal is meant to be tangible.
Some of our most fruitful gains are within.

| I AM *GRATEFUL* FOR ... | DATE: |
|---|---|

1. _____
2. _____
3. _____

| I AM *GRATEFUL* FOR ... | DATE: |
|---|---|

1. _____
2. _____
3. _____

| I AM *GRATEFUL* FOR ... | DATE: |
|---|---|

1. _____
2. _____
3. _____

| I AM *GRATEFUL* FOR ... | DATE: |
|---|---|

1. _____
2. _____
3. _____

| I AM *GRATEFUL* FOR ... | DATE: |
|---|---|

1. _____
2. _____
3. _____

| I AM *GRATEFUL* FOR ... | DATE: |
|---|---|

1. _____
2. _____
3. _____

| I AM *GRATEFUL* FOR ... | DATE: |
|---|---|

1. _____
2. _____
3. _____

# I AM A WORK IN PROGRESS AND CURRENTLY ON THE PURSUIT OF PEACE AND NOT JUST HAPPINESS.

---

Your faith must be stronger than your fear of not getting what you want.

| I AM *GRATEFUL* FOR ... | DATE: |
|---|---|

1. _____
2. _____
3. _____

| I AM *GRATEFUL* FOR ... | DATE: |
|---|---|

1. _____
2. _____
3. _____

| I AM *GRATEFUL* FOR ... | DATE: |
|---|---|

1. _____
2. _____
3. _____

| I AM *GRATEFUL* FOR … | DATE: |
|---|---|

1. _____
2. _____
3. _____

| I AM *GRATEFUL* FOR … | DATE: |
|---|---|

1. _____
2. _____
3. _____

| I AM *GRATEFUL* FOR … | DATE: |
|---|---|

1. _____
2. _____
3. _____

| I AM *GRATEFUL* FOR … | DATE: |
|---|---|

1. _____
2. _____
3. _____

# I AM A WORK IN PROGRESS AND CURRENTLY ON THE PURSUIT OF PEACE AND NOT JUST HAPPINESS.

We all flourish at different periods. During times of transition, we must learn to also celebrate the grey moments of our existence (the in-between).

| I AM *GRATEFUL* FOR … | DATE: |
|---|---|

1. _____
2. _____
3. _____

| I AM *GRATEFUL* FOR … | DATE: |
|---|---|

1. _____
2. _____
3. _____

| I AM *GRATEFUL* FOR … | DATE: |
|---|---|

1. _____
2. _____
3. _____

| I AM *GRATEFUL* FOR ... | DATE: |
|---|---|

1. _____
2. _____
3. _____

| I AM *GRATEFUL* FOR ... | DATE: |
|---|---|

1. _____
2. _____
3. _____

| I AM *GRATEFUL* FOR ... | DATE: |
|---|---|

1. _____
2. _____
3. _____

| I AM *GRATEFUL* FOR ... | DATE: |
|---|---|

1. _____
2. _____
3. _____

# I AM A WORK IN PROGRESS AND CURRENTLY ON THE PURSUIT OF PEACE AND NOT JUST HAPPINESS.

With hardship comes lessons, and lessons lead to growth, hopefully. These, in turn, create a complete, yet everblooming individual.

| I AM *GRATEFUL* FOR … | DATE: |
|---|---|

1. _____
2. _____
3. _____

| I AM *GRATEFUL* FOR … | DATE: |
|---|---|

1. _____
2. _____
3. _____

| I AM *GRATEFUL* FOR … | DATE: |
|---|---|

1. _____
2. _____
3. _____

| I AM *GRATEFUL* FOR ... | DATE: |
|---|---|

1. _____
2. _____
3. _____

| I AM *GRATEFUL* FOR ... | DATE: |
|---|---|

1. _____
2. _____
3. _____

| I AM *GRATEFUL* FOR ... | DATE: |
|---|---|

1. _____
2. _____
3. _____

| I AM *GRATEFUL* FOR ... | DATE: |
|---|---|

1. _____
2. _____
3. _____

RESET.

RELAX.

RECHARGE.

# WHAT ARE YOUR TOP 3 FAVORITE SELF-HELP BOOKS?

(READ THEM AGAIN)

_____

_____

_____

_____

_____

_____

_____

_____

_____

_____

_____

_____

_____

_____

_____

_____

_____

# I AM A WORK IN PROGRESS AND CURRENTLY ON THE PURSUIT OF PEACE AND NOT JUST HAPPINESS.

---

Surrender the many reasons you make up in your mind that inevitably prolong your greatness.

| I AM *GRATEFUL* FOR … | DATE: |
|---|---|

1. _____
2. _____
3. _____

| I AM *GRATEFUL* FOR … | DATE: |
|---|---|

1. _____
2. _____
3. _____

| I AM *GRATEFUL* FOR … | DATE: |
|---|---|

1. _____
2. _____
3. _____

| I AM *GRATEFUL* FOR ... | DATE: |
|---|---|

1. _____
2. _____
3. _____

| I AM *GRATEFUL* FOR ... | DATE: |
|---|---|

1. _____
2. _____
3. _____

| I AM *GRATEFUL* FOR ... | DATE: |
|---|---|

1. _____
2. _____
3. _____

| I AM *GRATEFUL* FOR ... | DATE: |
|---|---|

1. _____
2. _____
3. _____

# I AM A WORK IN PROGRESS AND CURRENTLY ON THE PURSUIT OF PEACE AND NOT JUST HAPPINESS.

---

Resilience over fear.

| I AM *GRATEFUL* FOR … | DATE: |
|---|---|

1. _____
2. _____
3. _____

| I AM *GRATEFUL* FOR … | DATE: |
|---|---|

1. _____
2. _____
3. _____

| I AM *GRATEFUL* FOR … | DATE: |
|---|---|

1. _____
2. _____
3. _____

| I AM *GRATEFUL* FOR … | DATE: |
|---|---|

1. _____

2. _____

3. _____

| I AM *GRATEFUL* FOR … | DATE: |
|---|---|

1. _____

2. _____

3. _____

| I AM *GRATEFUL* FOR … | DATE: |
|---|---|

1. _____

2. _____

3. _____

| I AM *GRATEFUL* FOR … | DATE: |
|---|---|

1. _____

2. _____

3. _____

# I AM A WORK IN PROGRESS AND CURRENTLY ON THE PURSUIT OF PEACE AND NOT JUST HAPPINESS.

---

Your reality is shaped by your choices. So it is important to be diligent about the steps we take in life.

| I AM *GRATEFUL* FOR ... | DATE: |
|---|---|

1. _____
2. _____
3. _____

| I AM *GRATEFUL* FOR ... | DATE: |
|---|---|

1. _____
2. _____
3. _____

| I AM *GRATEFUL* FOR ... | DATE: |
|---|---|

1. _____
2. _____
3. _____

| I AM *GRATEFUL* FOR ... | DATE: |
|---|---|

1. _____
2. _____
3. _____

| I AM *GRATEFUL* FOR ... | DATE: |
|---|---|

1. _____
2. _____
3. _____

| I AM *GRATEFUL* FOR ... | DATE: |
|---|---|

1. _____
2. _____
3. _____

| I AM *GRATEFUL* FOR ... | DATE: |
|---|---|

1. _____
2. _____
3. _____

# I AM A WORK IN PROGRESS AND CURRENTLY ON THE PURSUIT OF PEACE AND NOT JUST HAPPINESS.

I truly believe it is NEVER too late to redirect your path. If you
WANT greater ... If you BELIEVE you deserve greater ...
then you must work hard to ACHIEVE greater, no matter the age.

| I AM *GRATEFUL* FOR ... | DATE: |
|---|---|

1. _____
2. _____
3. _____

| I AM *GRATEFUL* FOR ... | DATE: |
|---|---|

1. _____
2. _____
3. _____

| I AM *GRATEFUL* FOR ... | DATE: |
|---|---|

1. _____
2. _____
3. _____

| I AM *GRATEFUL* FOR … | DATE: |
|---|---|

1. _____
2. _____
3. _____

| I AM *GRATEFUL* FOR … | DATE: |
|---|---|

1. _____
2. _____
3. _____

| I AM *GRATEFUL* FOR … | DATE: |
|---|---|

1. _____
2. _____
3. _____

| I AM *GRATEFUL* FOR … | DATE: |
|---|---|

1. _____
2. _____
3. _____

THERE IS
ENOUGH SUCCESS
FOR US ALL
THAT CHOOSE TO
PUT IN
THE WORK.

# WHAT ARE THREE OF YOUR MAJOR STRENGTHS?

# I AM A WORK IN PROGRESS AND CURRENTLY ON THE PURSUIT OF PEACE AND NOT JUST HAPPINESS.

---

All major shifts and enlightenment require mistakes, uncomfortable situations, sacrifice, long nights, etc. But true growth starts from within. Once the mind is right, the rest will follow.

| I AM *GRATEFUL* FOR … | DATE: |
|---|---|

1. _____
2. _____
3. _____

| I AM *GRATEFUL* FOR … | DATE: |
|---|---|

1. _____
2. _____
3. _____

| I AM *GRATEFUL* FOR … | DATE: |
|---|---|

1. _____
2. _____
3. _____

| I AM *GRATEFUL* FOR … | DATE: |
|---|---|

1. _____
2. _____
3. _____

| I AM *GRATEFUL* FOR … | DATE: |
|---|---|

1. _____
2. _____
3. _____

| I AM *GRATEFUL* FOR … | DATE: |
|---|---|

1. _____
2. _____
3. _____

| I AM *GRATEFUL* FOR … | DATE: |
|---|---|

1. _____
2. _____
3. _____

# I AM A WORK IN PROGRESS AND CURRENTLY ON THE PURSUIT OF PEACE AND NOT JUST HAPPINESS.

---

If you work hard enough, what's meant for us will always fall into our laps.

| I AM *GRATEFUL* FOR … | DATE: |
|---|---|

1. _____
2. _____
3. _____

| I AM *GRATEFUL* FOR … | DATE: |
|---|---|

1. _____
2. _____
3. _____

| I AM *GRATEFUL* FOR … | DATE: |
|---|---|

1. _____
2. _____
3. _____

| I AM *GRATEFUL* FOR ... | DATE: |
|---|---|

1. _____
2. _____
3. _____

| I AM *GRATEFUL* FOR ... | DATE: |
|---|---|

1. _____
2. _____
3. _____

| I AM *GRATEFUL* FOR ... | DATE: |
|---|---|

1. _____
2. _____
3. _____

| I AM *GRATEFUL* FOR ... | DATE: |
|---|---|

1. _____
2. _____
3. _____

# I AM A WORK IN PROGRESS AND CURRENTLY ON THE PURSUIT OF PEACE AND NOT JUST HAPPINESS.

---

Outside competition is obsolete because you're only truly competing against your own false limitations.

| I AM *GRATEFUL* FOR … | DATE: |
|---|---|

1. _____
2. _____
3. _____

| I AM *GRATEFUL* FOR … | DATE: |
|---|---|

1. _____
2. _____
3. _____

| I AM *GRATEFUL* FOR … | DATE: |
|---|---|

1. _____
2. _____
3. _____

| I AM *GRATEFUL* FOR ... | DATE: |
|---|---|

1. _____
2. _____
3. _____

| I AM *GRATEFUL* FOR ... | DATE: |
|---|---|

1. _____
2. _____
3. _____

| I AM *GRATEFUL* FOR ... | DATE: |
|---|---|

1. _____
2. _____
3. _____

| I AM *GRATEFUL* FOR ... | DATE: |
|---|---|

1. _____
2. _____
3. _____

# I AM A WORK IN PROGRESS AND CURRENTLY ON THE PURSUIT OF PEACE AND NOT JUST HAPPINESS.

---

Temporary fear is a part of the process, but you cannot live there.
Remember, you owe yourself the opportunity to flourish.

| I AM *GRATEFUL* FOR ... | DATE: |
|---|---|

1. _____
2. _____
3. _____

| I AM *GRATEFUL* FOR ... | DATE: |
|---|---|

1. _____
2. _____
3. _____

| I AM *GRATEFUL* FOR ... | DATE: |
|---|---|

1. _____
2. _____
3. _____

| I AM *GRATEFUL* FOR … | DATE: |
| --- | --- |

1. _____
2. _____
3. _____

| I AM *GRATEFUL* FOR … | DATE: |
| --- | --- |

1. _____
2. _____
3. _____

| I AM *GRATEFUL* FOR … | DATE: |
| --- | --- |

1. _____
2. _____
3. _____

| I AM *GRATEFUL* FOR … | DATE: |
| --- | --- |

1. _____
2. _____
3. _____

EVERYTHING
WE DESIRE
IS ON THE
OTHER SIDE
OF OUR
FIXED MINDSET.

# WHAT ARE THREE EXPERIENCES THAT HAVE HELPED MOLD YOU INTO THE INDIVIDUAL YOU ARE TODAY?

_____

_____

_____

_____

_____

_____

_____

_____

_____

_____

_____

_____

_____

_____

_____

_____

_____

_____

# I AM A WORK IN PROGRESS AND CURRENTLY ON THE PURSUIT OF PEACE AND NOT JUST HAPPINESS.

---

Continuously feeding self-doubt and replaying false failed scenarios in your head only create a stagnant existence. As hard as it may be to leap, jump head-first, and only look back to see how far you've come.

| I AM *GRATEFUL* FOR ... | DATE: |
|---|---|

1. _____
2. _____
3. _____

| I AM *GRATEFUL* FOR ... | DATE: |
|---|---|

1. _____
2. _____
3. _____

| I AM *GRATEFUL* FOR ... | DATE: |
|---|---|

1. _____
2. _____
3. _____

| I AM *GRATEFUL* FOR ... | DATE: |
|---|---|

1. _____
2. _____
3. _____

| I AM *GRATEFUL* FOR ... | DATE: |
|---|---|

1. _____
2. _____
3. _____

| I AM *GRATEFUL* FOR ... | DATE: |
|---|---|

1. _____
2. _____
3. _____

| I AM *GRATEFUL* FOR ... | DATE: |
|---|---|

1. _____
2. _____
3. _____

# I AM A WORK IN PROGRESS AND CURRENTLY ON THE PURSUIT OF PEACE AND NOT JUST HAPPINESS.

---

We don't exist to please everyone ...
We exist to inspire, motivate, and support whatever supports us.

| I AM *GRATEFUL* FOR ... | DATE: |
|---|---|

1. _____
2. _____
3. _____

| I AM *GRATEFUL* FOR ... | DATE: |
|---|---|

1. _____
2. _____
3. _____

| I AM *GRATEFUL* FOR ... | DATE: |
|---|---|

1. _____
2. _____
3. _____

| I AM *GRATEFUL* FOR ... | DATE: |
|---|---|

1. _____
2. _____
3. _____

| I AM *GRATEFUL* FOR ... | DATE: |
|---|---|

1. _____
2. _____
3. _____

| I AM *GRATEFUL* FOR ... | DATE: |
|---|---|

1. _____
2. _____
3. _____

| I AM *GRATEFUL* FOR ... | DATE: |
|---|---|

1. _____
2. _____
3. _____

# I AM A WORK IN PROGRESS AND CURRENTLY ON THE PURSUIT OF PEACE AND NOT JUST HAPPINESS.

---

I'm here to remind you not to be your own worst enemy.

| I AM *GRATEFUL* FOR … | DATE: |
|---|---|

1. _____
2. _____
3. _____

| I AM *GRATEFUL* FOR … | DATE: |
|---|---|

1. _____
2. _____
3. _____

| I AM *GRATEFUL* FOR … | DATE: |
|---|---|

1. _____
2. _____
3. _____

| I AM *GRATEFUL* FOR ... | DATE: |
|---|---|

1. _____
2. _____
3. _____

| I AM *GRATEFUL* FOR ... | DATE: |
|---|---|

1. _____
2. _____
3. _____

| I AM *GRATEFUL* FOR ... | DATE: |
|---|---|

1. _____
2. _____
3. _____

| I AM *GRATEFUL* FOR ... | DATE: |
|---|---|

1. _____
2. _____
3. _____

# I AM A WORK IN PROGRESS AND CURRENTLY ON THE PURSUIT OF PEACE AND NOT JUST HAPPINESS.

---

You want it? Work for it ...
You love it? It'll love you back with the right amount of nurture.

| I AM *GRATEFUL* FOR ... | DATE: |
|---|---|

1. _____
2. _____
3. _____

| I AM *GRATEFUL* FOR ... | DATE: |
|---|---|

1. _____
2. _____
3. _____

| I AM *GRATEFUL* FOR ... | DATE: |
|---|---|

1. _____
2. _____
3. _____

| I AM *GRATEFUL* FOR ... | DATE: |
|---|---|

1. _____
2. _____
3. _____

| I AM *GRATEFUL* FOR ... | DATE: |
|---|---|

1. _____
2. _____
3. _____

| I AM *GRATEFUL* FOR ... | DATE: |
|---|---|

1. _____
2. _____
3. _____

| I AM *GRATEFUL* FOR ... | DATE: |
|---|---|

1. _____
2. _____
3. _____

YOU

GOT

THIS

# WHAT ARE YOUR TOP 3 FAVORITE SCENTS THAT TAKE YOU TO YOUR *"HAPPY PLACE"*?

(THINK OF THEM OFTEN)

# I AM A WORK IN PROGRESS AND CURRENTLY ON THE PURSUIT OF PEACE AND NOT JUST HAPPINESS.

---

You know you got this, right? The key is to push through. To be stronger than our false thoughts, anxieties, and what we think we lack.

| I AM *GRATEFUL* FOR ... | DATE: |
|---|---|

1. _____
2. _____
3. _____

| I AM *GRATEFUL* FOR ... | DATE: |
|---|---|

1. _____
2. _____
3. _____

| I AM *GRATEFUL* FOR ... | DATE: |
|---|---|

1. _____
2. _____
3. _____

| I AM *GRATEFUL* FOR ... | DATE: |
|---|---|

1. _____
2. _____
3. _____

| I AM *GRATEFUL* FOR ... | DATE: |
|---|---|

1. _____
2. _____
3. _____

| I AM *GRATEFUL* FOR ... | DATE: |
|---|---|

1. _____
2. _____
3. _____

| I AM *GRATEFUL* FOR ... | DATE: |
|---|---|

1. _____
2. _____
3. _____

# I AM A WORK IN PROGRESS AND CURRENTLY ON THE PURSUIT OF PEACE AND NOT JUST HAPPINESS.

No amount of worry, guilt, or force will help us
achieve our goals any quicker.

| I AM *GRATEFUL* FOR … | DATE: |
|---|---|

1. _____
2. _____
3. _____

| I AM *GRATEFUL* FOR … | DATE: |
|---|---|

1. _____
2. _____
3. _____

| I AM *GRATEFUL* FOR … | DATE: |
|---|---|

1. _____
2. _____
3. _____

| I AM *GRATEFUL* FOR ... | DATE: |
|---|---|

1. _____
2. _____
3. _____

| I AM *GRATEFUL* FOR ... | DATE: |
|---|---|

1. _____
2. _____
3. _____

| I AM *GRATEFUL* FOR ... | DATE: |
|---|---|

1. _____
2. _____
3. _____

| I AM *GRATEFUL* FOR ... | DATE: |
|---|---|

1. _____
2. _____
3. _____

# I AM A WORK IN PROGRESS AND CURRENTLY ON THE PURSUIT OF PEACE AND NOT JUST HAPPINESS.

You're not a failure ... You're just simply in the process of your desired objective and everything it entails.

| I AM *GRATEFUL* FOR ... | DATE: |
|---|---|

1. _____
2. _____
3. _____

| I AM *GRATEFUL* FOR ... | DATE: |
|---|---|

1. _____
2. _____
3. _____

| I AM *GRATEFUL* FOR ... | DATE: |
|---|---|

1. _____
2. _____
3. _____

| I AM *GRATEFUL* FOR ... | DATE: |
|---|---|

1. _____
2. _____
3. _____

| I AM *GRATEFUL* FOR ... | DATE: |
|---|---|

1. _____
2. _____
3. _____

| I AM *GRATEFUL* FOR ... | DATE: |
|---|---|

1. _____
2. _____
3. _____

| I AM *GRATEFUL* FOR ... | DATE: |
|---|---|

1. _____
2. _____
3. _____

# I AM A WORK IN PROGRESS AND CURRENTLY ON THE PURSUIT OF PEACE AND NOT JUST HAPPINESS.

---

We ALL have the capability to become our best selves.
The determining factor is how much hard work and dedication
we are willing to put into our spirit.

| I AM *GRATEFUL* FOR ... | DATE: |
|---|---|

1. _____
2. _____
3. _____

| I AM *GRATEFUL* FOR ... | DATE: |
|---|---|

1. _____
2. _____
3. _____

| I AM *GRATEFUL* FOR ... | DATE: |
|---|---|

1. _____
2. _____
3. _____

| I AM *GRATEFUL* FOR ... | DATE: |
|---|---|

1. _____
2. _____
3. _____

| I AM *GRATEFUL* FOR ... | DATE: |
|---|---|

1. _____
2. _____
3. _____

| I AM *GRATEFUL* FOR ... | DATE: |
|---|---|

1. _____
2. _____
3. _____

| I AM *GRATEFUL* FOR ... | DATE: |
|---|---|

1. _____
2. _____
3. _____

WE ARE ALL
A WORK
IN PROGRESS;
PERFECTLY
IMPERFECT BEINGS,
FLAWED BUT
NEVER BROKEN.

# WHAT IS YOUR PURPOSE, AND WHAT IS STOPPING YOU FROM PURSUING IT?

# I AM A WORK IN PROGRESS AND CURRENTLY ON THE PURSUIT OF PEACE AND NOT JUST HAPPINESS.

---

Take a moment. Close your eyes. Give thanks to how far you've come.
How much you've transformed. And how much you're still evolving DAILY.

| I AM *GRATEFUL* FOR ... | DATE: |
|---|---|

1. _____
2. _____
3. _____

| I AM *GRATEFUL* FOR ... | DATE: |
|---|---|

1. _____
2. _____
3. _____

| I AM *GRATEFUL* FOR ... | DATE: |
|---|---|

1. _____
2. _____
3. _____

| I AM *GRATEFUL* FOR ... | DATE: |
|---|---|

1. _____
2. _____
3. _____

| I AM *GRATEFUL* FOR ... | DATE: |
|---|---|

1. _____
2. _____
3. _____

| I AM *GRATEFUL* FOR ... | DATE: |
|---|---|

1. _____
2. _____
3. _____

| I AM *GRATEFUL* FOR ... | DATE: |
|---|---|

1. _____
2. _____
3. _____

# I AM A WORK IN PROGRESS AND CURRENTLY ON THE PURSUIT OF PEACE AND NOT JUST HAPPINESS.

Put the work in 'til it works out.

| I AM *GRATEFUL* FOR … | DATE: |
|---|---|

1. _____
2. _____
3. _____

| I AM *GRATEFUL* FOR … | DATE: |
|---|---|

1. _____
2. _____
3. _____

| I AM *GRATEFUL* FOR … | DATE: |
|---|---|

1. _____
2. _____
3. _____

| I AM *GRATEFUL* FOR ... | DATE: |
|---|---|

1. _____
2. _____
3. _____

| I AM *GRATEFUL* FOR ... | DATE: |
|---|---|

1. _____
2. _____
3. _____

| I AM *GRATEFUL* FOR ... | DATE: |
|---|---|

1. _____
2. _____
3. _____

| I AM *GRATEFUL* FOR ... | DATE: |
|---|---|

1. _____
2. _____
3. _____

# I AM A WORK IN PROGRESS AND CURRENTLY ON THE PURSUIT OF PEACE AND NOT JUST HAPPINESS.

---

The road to self-discipline is not an easy one. The first step is to identify our strengths and weaknesses when it comes to consistently taking control of our actions—which inevitably excel our future.

| I AM *GRATEFUL* FOR ... | DATE: |
|---|---|

1. _____
2. _____
3. _____

| I AM *GRATEFUL* FOR ... | DATE: |
|---|---|

1. _____
2. _____
3. _____

| I AM *GRATEFUL* FOR ... | DATE: |
|---|---|

1. _____
2. _____
3. _____

| I AM *GRATEFUL* FOR … | DATE: |
|---|---|

1. _____
2. _____
3. _____

| I AM *GRATEFUL* FOR … | DATE: |
|---|---|

1. _____
2. _____
3. _____

| I AM *GRATEFUL* FOR … | DATE: |
|---|---|

1. _____
2. _____
3. _____

| I AM *GRATEFUL* FOR … | DATE: |
|---|---|

1. _____
2. _____
3. _____

# I AM A WORK IN PROGRESS AND CURRENTLY ON THE PURSUIT OF PEACE AND NOT JUST HAPPINESS.

Remember, it's so important to celebrate ALL triumphs.
Recognizing and appreciating our victories only attracts more.

| I AM *GRATEFUL* FOR … | DATE: |
|---|---|

1. _____
2. _____
3. _____

| I AM *GRATEFUL* FOR … | DATE: |
|---|---|

1. _____
2. _____
3. _____

| I AM *GRATEFUL* FOR … | DATE: |
|---|---|

1. _____
2. _____
3. _____

| I AM *GRATEFUL* FOR … | DATE: |
|---|---|

1. _____
2. _____
3. _____

| I AM *GRATEFUL* FOR … | DATE: |
|---|---|

1. _____
2. _____
3. _____

| I AM *GRATEFUL* FOR … | DATE: |
|---|---|

1. _____
2. _____
3. _____

| I AM *GRATEFUL* FOR … | DATE: |
|---|---|

1. _____
2. _____
3. _____

WHEN WE BUILD
EACH OTHER UP,
IT CREATES
INCLUSIVITY AND
OPPORTUNITY
WE OTHERWISE
WOULD NOT BE
OPEN TO.

# WHAT ARE THE THREE SONGS
# THAT GET YOU HYPED?

(PLAY THOSE DAILY)

---

_____

_____

_____

_____

_____

_____

_____

_____

_____

_____

_____

_____

_____

_____

_____

_____

_____

# I AM A WORK IN PROGRESS AND CURRENTLY ON THE PURSUIT OF PEACE AND NOT JUST HAPPINESS.

---

*Self-love ebbs and flows, and requires nurture throughout every stage of our lives.*

| I AM *GRATEFUL* FOR ... | DATE: |
|---|---|

1. _____
2. _____
3. _____

| I AM *GRATEFUL* FOR ... | DATE: |
|---|---|

1. _____
2. _____
3. _____

| I AM *GRATEFUL* FOR ... | DATE: |
|---|---|

1. _____
2. _____
3. _____

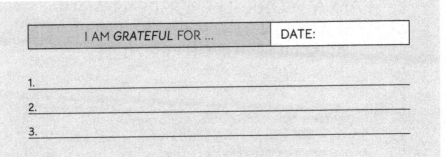

| I AM *GRATEFUL* FOR ... | DATE: |

1. _____
2. _____
3. _____

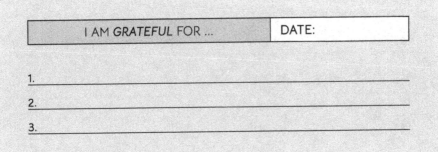

| I AM *GRATEFUL* FOR ... | DATE: |

1. _____
2. _____
3. _____

| I AM *GRATEFUL* FOR ... | DATE: |

1. _____
2. _____
3. _____

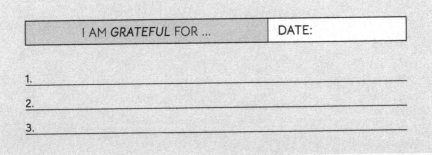

| I AM *GRATEFUL* FOR ... | DATE: |

1. _____
2. _____
3. _____

# I AM A WORK IN PROGRESS AND CURRENTLY ON THE PURSUIT OF PEACE AND NOT JUST HAPPINESS.

When busy work is taking precedence over productivity that will actually further your future, it's time to re-evaluate why we are avoiding the real work at hand.

| I AM *GRATEFUL* FOR ... | DATE: |
|---|---|

1. _____
2. _____
3. _____

| I AM *GRATEFUL* FOR ... | DATE: |
|---|---|

1. _____
2. _____
3. _____

| I AM *GRATEFUL* FOR ... | DATE: |
|---|---|

1. _____
2. _____
3. _____

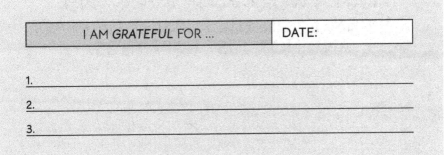

| I AM *GRATEFUL* FOR ... | DATE: |
|---|---|

1. _____
2. _____
3. _____

| I AM *GRATEFUL* FOR ... | DATE: |
|---|---|

1. _____
2. _____
3. _____

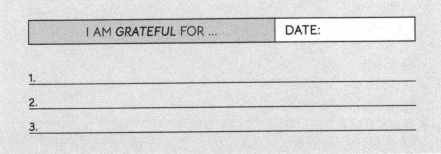

| I AM *GRATEFUL* FOR ... | DATE: |
|---|---|

1. _____
2. _____
3. _____

| I AM *GRATEFUL* FOR ... | DATE: |
|---|---|

1. _____
2. _____
3. _____

# I AM A WORK IN PROGRESS AND CURRENTLY ON THE PURSUIT OF PEACE AND NOT JUST HAPPINESS.

Fear of failure? Fear of success? Lack of confidence/motivation?
Whatever the case, YOU GOT THIS!

| I AM *GRATEFUL* FOR ... | DATE: |
|---|---|

1. _____
2. _____
3. _____

| I AM *GRATEFUL* FOR ... | DATE: |
|---|---|

1. _____
2. _____
3. _____

| I AM *GRATEFUL* FOR ... | DATE: |
|---|---|

1. _____
2. _____
3. _____

| I AM *GRATEFUL* FOR … | DATE: |
|---|---|

1. _____
2. _____
3. _____

| I AM *GRATEFUL* FOR … | DATE: |
|---|---|

1. _____
2. _____
3. _____

| I AM *GRATEFUL* FOR … | DATE: |
|---|---|

1. _____
2. _____
3. _____

| I AM *GRATEFUL* FOR … | DATE: |
|---|---|

1. _____
2. _____
3. _____

# I AM A WORK IN PROGRESS AND CURRENTLY ON THE PURSUIT OF PEACE AND NOT JUST HAPPINESS.

Compassion over criticism.

| I AM *GRATEFUL* FOR ... | DATE: |
|---|---|

1. _____
2. _____
3. _____

| I AM *GRATEFUL* FOR ... | DATE: |
|---|---|

1. _____
2. _____
3. _____

| I AM *GRATEFUL* FOR ... | DATE: |
|---|---|

1. _____
2. _____
3. _____

| I AM *GRATEFUL* FOR … | DATE: |
|---|---|

1. _____
2. _____
3. _____

| I AM *GRATEFUL* FOR … | DATE: |
|---|---|

1. _____
2. _____
3. _____

| I AM *GRATEFUL* FOR … | DATE: |
|---|---|

1. _____
2. _____
3. _____

| I AM *GRATEFUL* FOR … | DATE: |
|---|---|

1. _____
2. _____
3. _____

WE ARE ALL A
WORK IN
PROGRESS
AND HOPEFULLY,
ON THE
PURSUIT OF PEACE
AND NOT JUST
HAPPINESS.

# WRITE DOWN THREE OF YOUR FAVORITE AFFIRMATIONS.

(RECITE THEM OUT LOUD DAILY)

---

---

---

---

---

---

---

---

---

---

---

---

---

---

---

---

---

---

---

---

# I AM A WORK IN PROGRESS AND CURRENTLY ON THE PURSUIT OF PEACE AND NOT JUST HAPPINESS.

---

Feel what you need to feel, but don't let it consume you.

| I AM *GRATEFUL* FOR ... | DATE: |
|---|---|

1. _____
2. _____
3. _____

| I AM *GRATEFUL* FOR ... | DATE: |
|---|---|

1. _____
2. _____
3. _____

| I AM *GRATEFUL* FOR ... | DATE: |
|---|---|

1. _____
2. _____
3. _____

| I AM *GRATEFUL* FOR ... | DATE: |
|---|---|

1. _____
2. _____
3. _____

| I AM *GRATEFUL* FOR ... | DATE: |
|---|---|

1. _____
2. _____
3. _____

| I AM *GRATEFUL* FOR ... | DATE: |
|---|---|

1. _____
2. _____
3. _____

| I AM *GRATEFUL* FOR ... | DATE: |
|---|---|

1. _____
2. _____
3. _____

# I AM A WORK IN PROGRESS AND CURRENTLY ON THE PURSUIT OF PEACE AND NOT JUST HAPPINESS.

---

You can still be strong, kindhearted & respected,
all while proving your point.

| I AM *GRATEFUL* FOR ... | DATE: |
|---|---|

1. _____
2. _____
3. _____

| I AM *GRATEFUL* FOR ... | DATE: |
|---|---|

1. _____
2. _____
3. _____

| I AM *GRATEFUL* FOR ... | DATE: |
|---|---|

1. _____
2. _____
3. _____

| I AM *GRATEFUL* FOR ... | DATE: |
|---|---|

1. _____
2. _____
3. _____

| I AM *GRATEFUL* FOR ... | DATE: |
|---|---|

1. _____
2. _____
3. _____

| I AM *GRATEFUL* FOR ... | DATE: |
|---|---|

1. _____
2. _____
3. _____

| I AM *GRATEFUL* FOR ... | DATE: |
|---|---|

1. _____
2. _____
3. _____

# I AM A WORK IN PROGRESS AND CURRENTLY ON THE PURSUIT OF PEACE AND NOT JUST HAPPINESS.

---

Emotional intelligence is an ever-evolving push through stagnation.

| I AM *GRATEFUL* FOR … | DATE: |
|---|---|

1. _____
2. _____
3. _____

| I AM *GRATEFUL* FOR … | DATE: |
|---|---|

1. _____
2. _____
3. _____

| I AM *GRATEFUL* FOR … | DATE: |
|---|---|

1. _____
2. _____
3. _____

| I AM *GRATEFUL* FOR … | DATE: |
|---|---|

1. _____
2. _____
3. _____

| I AM *GRATEFUL* FOR … | DATE: |
|---|---|

1. _____
2. _____
3. _____

| I AM *GRATEFUL* FOR … | DATE: |
|---|---|

1. _____
2. _____
3. _____

| I AM *GRATEFUL* FOR … | DATE: |
|---|---|

1. _____
2. _____
3. _____

# I AM A WORK IN PROGRESS AND CURRENTLY ON THE PURSUIT OF PEACE AND NOT JUST HAPPINESS.

When we create peace, harmony, and balance in our minds,
we will find it in our lives—and everything else we want and work towards.

| I AM *GRATEFUL* FOR ... | DATE: |
|---|---|

1. _____
2. _____
3. _____

| I AM *GRATEFUL* FOR ... | DATE: |
|---|---|

1. _____
2. _____
3. _____

| I AM *GRATEFUL* FOR ... | DATE: |
|---|---|

1. _____
2. _____
3. _____

| I AM *GRATEFUL* FOR ... | DATE: |
|---|---|

1. _____
2. _____
3. _____

| I AM *GRATEFUL* FOR ... | DATE: |
|---|---|

1. _____
2. _____
3. _____

| I AM *GRATEFUL* FOR ... | DATE: |
|---|---|

1. _____
2. _____
3. _____

| I AM *GRATEFUL* FOR ... | DATE: |
|---|---|

1. _____
2. _____
3. _____

# YEAR-END AFFIRMATION.

I am honoring the present.

Implementing boundaries.

Restoring energy.

Remaining focused.

Working hard.

Taking guilt-free breaks when need be.

Humble yet not hesitant to shine.

Evolving at my own pace.

**I AM GRATEFUL.**

A POST HILL PRESS BOOK
ISBN: 978-1-63758-251-0

The Art of Gratitude:
3 Minute Morning Ritual Journal
© 2022 by Nazanin Mandi
All Rights Reserved

Journal design by Álvaro Guzman.

Post Hill Press
New York · Nashville
posthillpress.com

Published in the United States of America
1 2 3 4 5 6 7 8 9 10

Nazanin